STAY ALIVE

A Transgender's Safety Guidebook

By: Grace Felicia Lawrence

GTS Global Transgender Safety Tasks Force USA Inc.

Copyright © 2021 Grace Felicia Lawrence
All rights reserved
First Edition

PAGE PUBLISHING, INC.
Conneaut Lake, PA

First originally published by Page Publishing 2021

ISBN 978-1-6624-5764-7 (pbk)
ISBN 978-1-6624-5765-4 (digital)

Printed in the United States of America

Global Transgender Safety Tasks Force USA INC

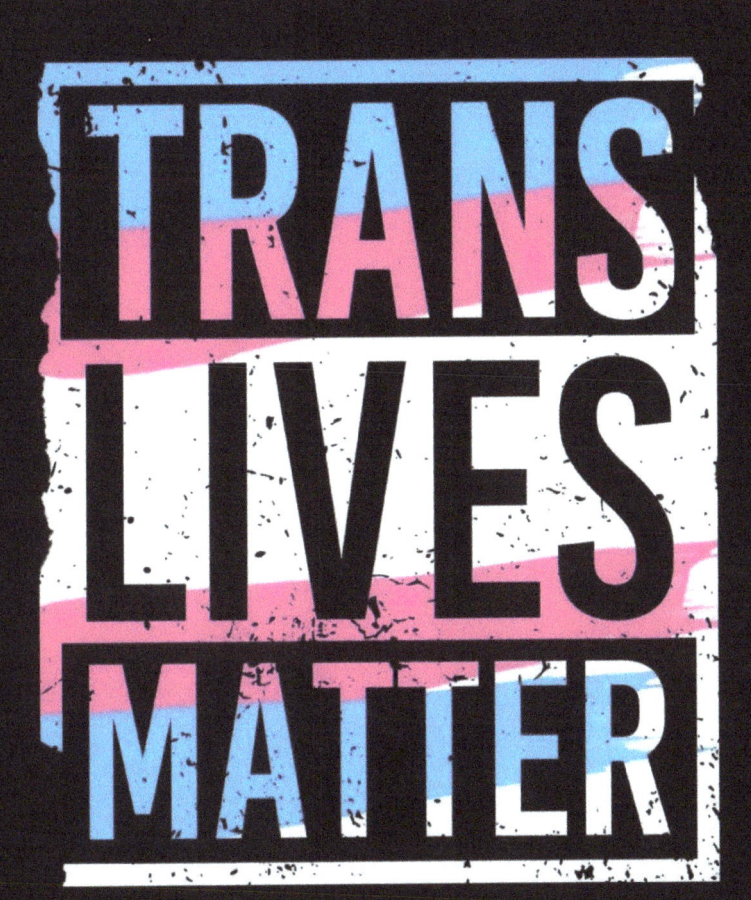

TRANS LIVES MATTER

01
CHAPTER ONE
History and Our Mission   7

02
CHAPTER TWO
COVID-19 and The Transgender Community   13

03
CHAPTER THREE
Sixteen Safety Tips That Will Keep You Alive as an Individual Transgender   16

04
CHAPTER FOUR
Grace's Personal Story
The Life and Struggle of a Transgender Immigrant *Grace Felicia Lawrence*   23

05
CHAPTER FIVE
Resources for The LGBTQ + Community   35

GTS Global Transgender Safety Tasks Force USA Inc.

01
CHAPTER ONE
History and Our Mission

Based on available statistics, every year on average, 368 transgender, queer, intersex, and other gender nonconforming people are killed worldwide due to their gender status. During the first ten months of 2018, at least 22 gender nonconforming people had been killed in the United States, 16 of them were people of color. The Global Transgender Safety Tasks Force USA Inc. (GTS) is a Californian nonprofit, tax-exempt, public benefit corporation strictly dedicated to the safety, security, and well-being of transgender and gender nonconforming people in the United States and around the world.

Accordingly, our mission is to promote safety by providing gender nonconforming people with books, materials, techniques, and training developed by experts to help them avoid dangerous situations and to protect themselves when avoidance isn't successful. We also intend to further educate the community on these topics through conferences held internationally. A vital part of our mission is to provide assistance—through professionals—to help gender nonconforming people living in countries where they are particularly at risk to relocate and seek asylum in countries that do not institutionalized discrimination and danger. GTS also intends to educate the public regarding the need for legal protections and equal rights for gender nonconforming people.

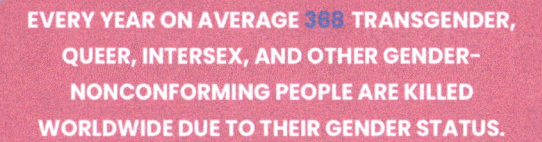

> **EVERY YEAR ON AVERAGE 368 TRANSGENDER, QUEER, INTERSEX, AND OTHER GENDER-NONCONFORMING PEOPLE ARE KILLED WORLDWIDE DUE TO THEIR GENDER STATUS.**

protect the gender nonconforming community.[1] As a longtime photojournalist, Ms. Lawrence has documented the plight of the community in Africa, the United States, and elsewhere. Having obtained asylum herself in the United States and then US citizenship, Ms. Lawrence has, for the past ten years, worked actively to help members of the community in Africa to escape the dangers they face in many countries there.

Ms. Lawrence is recognized as a leader of the gender nonconforming community. Ms. Lawrence appeared in the documentary film *Major!* which details the life and work of pioneering trans woman, Ms. Major. Ms. Lawrence was also honored to be selected as one of two Grand

---

[1] In the first attack, Ms. Lawrence was shot in the head (the bullet remains embedded); in the second, she was doused with battery acid, creating extensive scarring; and in the third, she was attacked by seven men bent on killing her.

Marshals of the 2018 Sacramento Pride Parade, an event that annually draws an audience of ten thousand to fifteen thousand people.

The GTS board of directors is highly diverse and includes professionals, members of the LGBTQ community, and people of color. GTS has strict nondiscrimination and nonviolence policies.

On August 30, 2018, GTS obtained IRC 501(c)(3), charitable nonprofit status, #36-4910216. References and more information are available upon request.

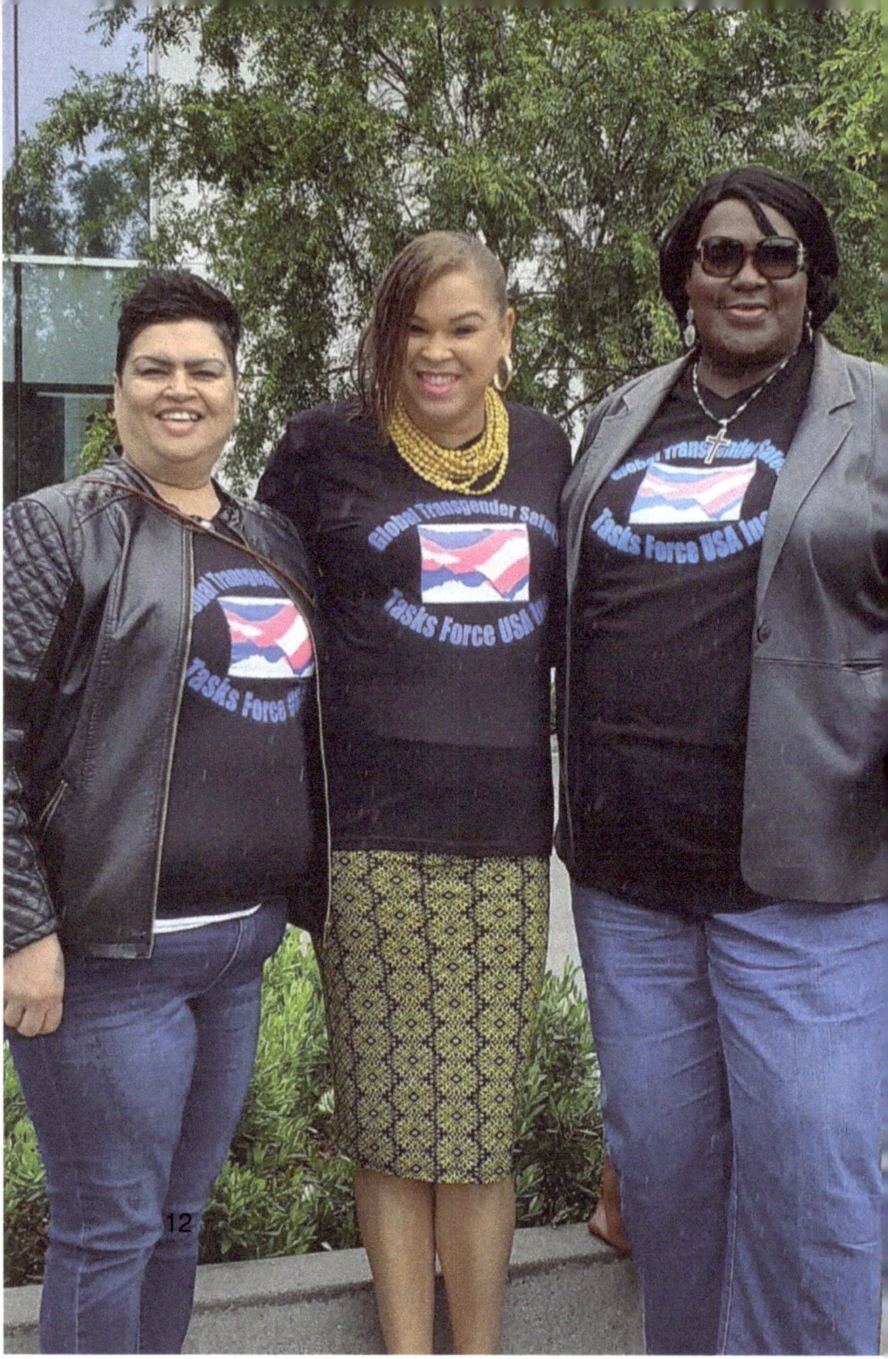
Global Transgender
Tasks Force USA Inc

GTS Global Transgender Safety Tasks Force USA Inc.

02
CHAPTER TWO
COVID-19 and The Transgender Community

IN THE BEST OF TIMES, THE LIVES, HEALTH, AND WELL-BEING OF TRANSGENDER AND NON-BINARY (TGNB) PEOPLE ARE PRECARIOUS. WITH THE COVID-19 PANDEMIC, THE PRESSURES HAVE INCREASED SIGNIFICANTLY, THUS **WORSENING** THEIR CONDITION.

The 2015 National Transgender Discrimination Survey found that TGNB people were unemployed at three times the rate of the general population and four times for TGNB people of color. Household incomes of TGNB people were found to be significantly lower than the general population, 12 percent reported annual income of less than $10,000. This economic instability results from a legacy of discrimination in education and employment, family rejection, and other pressures. As a result, the risk of the coronavirus infection increased, and the outcome of the infection is worse than that of the general population. Moreover, access to nonemergency medical care has been restricted, thus preventing TGNB people from getting the care needed to help with dysphoria.[2]

---

[2] Julie Woulfe and Melina Wald, "The Impact of the COVID-19 Pandemic on the Transgender and Nonbinary Community" (Columbia University, Department of Psychiatry, 2020).

Social isolation—while they are often quarantined with others who disapprove of their status—exacerbates emotional and mental health problems and may result in increased self-harm.

With lockdowns and quarantines, as well as unemployment, the risk of domestic violence increased. In all of 2019, twenty-six TGNB people were murdered; in 2020, twenty-eight were murdered in the first eight months.[3] More incidents of violence and murder are regrettably expected.

As a largely marginalized population, TGNB people are disproportionately impacted by the pandemic, which places them at greater risk of further marginalization, danger, poverty, and harm.

---

[3] Ibid.

GTS Global Transgender Safety Tasks Force USA Inc.

03
CHAPTER THREE
Sixteen Safety Tips That Will Keep You Alive as an Individual Transgender

1. Never go somewhere private with someone you just met. Stay in public places that are well lit and busy.

2. Be completely upfront and honest with the person regarding your trans or gender nonconforming status.

3. After you have gotten to know someone better and they you (following rules 1 and 2) and before going into private places, introduce the person to a friend, coworker, or loved one in a public place.

4. Agree on place to meet privately and inform a friend or loved one where you are going and when you expect to return or check in with

the friend or loved one. Stick to the plan—do not change locations.

5. When traveling, be sure to follow all these rules and avoid random hookups. You are at a higher risk in locations where you may not be familiar with a local culture of intolerance, such as certain regions in the country and internationally, and where there may be few or no resources to help and protect trans people.

6. If you experience a relationship breakup, avoid attempts to "out" your former partner or otherwise seek personal retaliation. If a crime was committed by your former

partner, report it to the authorities where and when safe to do so.

7. Consider using rideshare in the evenings instead of walking long distances. Social service agencies often provide bus passes or gift cards to Uber/Lyft for clients.

8. Sign up for a free self-defense class. There is a lot to learn about common methods attackers take.

9. In a tech era, it is common for many people to wear earphones, but it's important to stay alert after dark or in unfamiliar parts of town.

10. Find your "safe spots" on your walking routes, perhaps a coffee shop, bar, or restaurant that is trans-affirming. If someone is following your or harassing you, you'll have a safe place to walk into.

11. Keep your keys in a separate place from your purse. In the event that your purse is stolen, you will not be stuck.

12. If you are housed, have a bright censored light outside. A small camera system can help identify if anyone is lingering around your place. This includes hookups!

13. Get on PrEP. Sexual health is important, and PrEP is the best way to protect yourself from HIV.

14. Carry a lawyer's business card with you. In the event that you are detained or arrested by the police, it's important that you have adequate representation.

15. If you are employed, inquire about inclusive policies to ensure your protection.

16. Memorize at least two phone numbers in case you are robbed or incarcerated, especially if your primary language is not English.

22

GTS Global Transgender Safety Tasks Force USA Inc.

04

CHAPTER FOUR
Grace's Personal Story

The Life and Struggle of a

Transgender Immigrant
Grace Felicia Lawrence

Most trans people—and I am no exception—have experienced difficult and often life-threatening hardships as we recognize our gender and attempt to live as we truly are. This book is intended to highlight many of those hardships and dangers and to suggest ways to avoid or minimize them.

As a start, allow me to explain my background and experiences that have led me to publish this book, which I hope will help you, the reader, to live a full and happy life, free of the many dangers that I and the others have had to endure. Some are surviving like me (I survived three extremely violent attacks) while sadly each year, many other trans people are killed.

I am Black, born in Liberia, West Africa. I was assigned at birth as a male—the eldest son of a prominent family—and was groomed in my early years to assume the role of eventual patriarch. Yet I knew within myself that I was different. Either gay or trans, it would have been life-threatening for me to declare myself openly there, as it still is in many parts of Africa and elsewhere to this day. So I kept it to myself.

My family eventually moved to the United States, in the upper Midwest. I continued my outward role, married a lovely woman, and had children. But I was becoming more and more uncomfortable with the dissonance between my outward life and my true inner self. Gripped by fear of the consequences, I nevertheless resolved to come out and tell my wife and family that I was in fact trans and would begin the transition to being a woman. I was in my thirties.

My fears were justified. When I told my mother that I was not just gay but considered myself to be a woman, she told me I was "crazy." All of my family declared that they didn't want to have anything to do with me and kicked me out.

With almost no resources, I moved to San Francisco, looking for a more accepting environment where I could start a new life. But at first, my experience in the city was hard. I began the expensive transition therapy and had to earn some basic support to live. At that time, I was an undocumented immigrant, so my options to earn any money were very limited. I could do nothing but work in the drug and sex industries, also eventually becoming a drug user. I lived in a residential "hotel" where the manager would double-lock the door to my room if I didn't have the night's rent paid by 6:00 p.m. I was on a downward spiral.

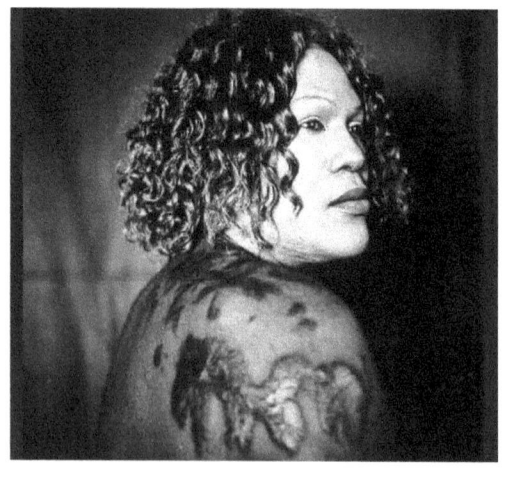

GRACE FELICIA LAWRENCE

The city wasn't a safe haven. Targeted because I am trans, I was shot in the head—the bullet is still there because it can't be surgically removed. Then later, I was attacked by someone who doused me with battery acid. Horrible and painful, I was disfigured by the attack. But thankfully, my face was able to be reconstructed surgically to remove most of the scarring.

Being six-foot three, Black, and trans, I was also often targeted by the police for arrest on various charges. Nearly all such cases were dismissed. I was convicted of only one charge, receiving stolen property (two computers I bought), which I didn't know were stolen.

While on probation for that conviction, I was attacked on the streets of San Francisco by seven homophobic/transphobic men. I defended myself, beat back the attackers, and put two in the hospital. But I was arrested and charged with probation violations. Though he expressed sympathy for the ordeals I had endured, the judge found I had violated my probation and sentenced me to jail based on my conviction for receiving stolen property. (I was not charged with independent crimes for having fought the attackers.)

After spending two months in jail, I was turned over to ICE for eventual deportation. I was in solitary confinement, ostensibly for my protection because of the frequency with which trans people are attacked in jail. I was let out of my cell one hour per day—but often that hour was in the evening, so usually I could not call my lawyer who was representing me in the deportation case. So I wrote her letter after letter and wrote to the judge presiding in the deportation case, pleading for asylum since being returned to Liberia would be a death sentence for me. I have seen gay people burned alive there.

I spent three years in custody awaiting possible deportation. I was taunted and harassed by other inmates all the time. The showers were particularly difficult. Twice it appeared I would be deported. Horrified and knowing that it would be my end if deported, twice I attempted suicide, but in both cases, I was (thankfully) saved by the guards.

But then, there was light at the end of the tunnel. Through my lawyer's efforts and the decision of the judge, I was granted asylum under the United Nations Convention against Torture, which had been ratified by the United States and is enforceable law. The judge wished me luck, words I cherished to this day.

Having been given asylum and the chance to stabilize and improve my life, I got a work permit and a driver's license and started working. Life is a learning experience, and I came to recognize that my own decisions contributed to the dangers I had experienced, so I began to communicate my experiences and perhaps wisdom to other trans people. I volunteered with the TGI Justice Project in San Francisco, providing guidance to other immigrant trans women, whether they were in or out of detention. I have also been fortunate enough, through the US State Department, to help other African LGBTQ people escape to the United States and Europe where asylum can be granted. To inspire other LGBTQ immigrants particularly, I have been invited to tell my story publicly to organizations and conventions around the United States. I have been involved with other LGBTQ organizations that raise funds for charity.

In 2018, I founded Global Transgender Safety Tasks Force USA Inc. (GTS), a Californian nonprofit corporation, which quickly was granted tax-exempt status under 501(c)(3) of the Internal Revenue Code, for the purpose of helping transgender and other gender nonconforming people to be safe and secure. To that end, GTS published a card we distributed to thousands of people to give our at-risk populations brief tips to improve safety, security, and well-being. This book is a more detailed reference guide intended to take the message and information throughout the state, nation, and world. I hope you found it helpful.

> **BE SAFE AND SECURE!**

34

CHAPTER FIVE
05
Resources for The LGBTQ + Community

RESOURCES

WORLD-WIDE

BTAC BLACK TRANS

Improves the Black trans human experience by overcoming violence and injustice in the world.

blacktrans.org

(646) 871-8022

GLAAD TRANSGENDER RESOURCES

GLAAD tackles tough issues to shape the narrative and provoke dialogue that leads to cultural change.

Glaad.org/transgender/resources

(855) 624-7715

NATIONAL (USA)

NATIONAL SUICIDE PREVENTION

It's 24-7, free and confidential support for people in distress, prevention, and crisis resources for you and your loved ones.

suicidepreventionlifeline.org

(800) 273-8255

THE TREVOR PROJECT

The leading national organization providing crisis intervention and suicide prevention services to LGBTQ+ people under twenty-five.

thetrevorproject.org

(866) 488-7386

NATIONAL TRANSGENDER EQUALITY

Advocates to change society to increase understanding and acceptance of transgender people.

transequality.org

(202) 642-454

SACRAMENTO GENDER HEALTH CENTER

Nonprofit organization and community clinic focusing on transgender health in Sacramento, California.

(916) 455-2391

genderhealthcenter.org

SACRAMENTO LGBTQA+ CENTER

Creating a region where LGBTQ+ people thrive means being an advocate for equity and social justice within and external to the LGBTQ+ community.

(916)442-0185

Saccenter.org/transgender-services

About the Author

Grace Felicia Lawrence is a West African, a three-time hate crime survivor, and the ONLY openly known transgender woman from Monrovia, Liberia, with asylum in the USA living in Sacramento, California. Grace Lawrence is the founder and president of the International Human Rights Nonprofit Organization and Global Transgender Safety Tasks Force USA Inc. Ms. Lawrence funds this organization to keep the transgender community safe around the world.

CPSIA information can be obtained
at www.ICGtesting.com
Printed in the USA
LVHW070305230822
726642LV00026B/667